Controversial Discussion Starters

By Stephen Parolini

Loveland, Colorado

Controversial Discussion Starters
Copyright © 1992 Stephen Parolini

Credits
Edited by Michael Warden
Designed by Dori Walker
Cover design by Bob Fuller and Liz Howe

Library of Congress Cataloging-in-Publication Data
Parolini, Stephen, 1959-
      Controversial discussion starters / by Stephen Parolini.
          p. cm.
      ISBN 1-55945-156-4
      1. Church group work with teenagers. 2. Theology, Doctrinal—Popular works. 3. Christian ethics—Popular works. I. Title.
      BV4447.P28 1992
      268'.433—dc20   92-35023
                                          CIP

ISBN 1-55945-156-4

12 11 10 9 8 7   04 03 02 01 00 99 98
Printed in the United States of America.

Dedication

To Gary and Vicki Camp for their
perseverance in youth ministry. And
to David Bump, whose "it depends"
inspired this book.

Contents

Part One: Discussion Starters
Faith Issues

Health Issues

Scientific and Medical Issues

Sexuality Issues

Social and Political Issues

Do the courts have the right to choose death as punishment for a serious crime?

Part Two: Bonus Discussion-Starter Activities

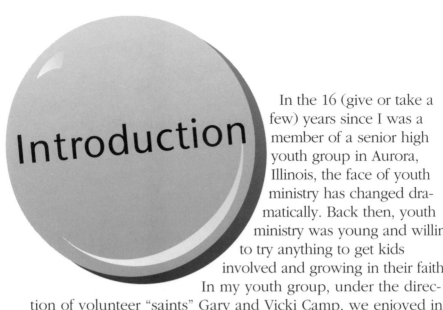

Introduction

In the 16 (give or take a few) years since I was a member of a senior high youth group in Aurora, Illinois, the face of youth ministry has changed dramatically. Back then, youth ministry was young and willing to try anything to get kids involved and growing in their faith. In my youth group, under the direction of volunteer "saints" Gary and Vicki Camp, we enjoyed in-depth Bible study, Frisbee golf, silly skits and lots of pizza. We traveled from Illinois to Colorado for a weeklong "mountaintop" experience. We went to a Christian music festival in Kentucky. We went on retreats and participated in simulation games. And, we had great discussions.

Today's youth ministry is more sophisticated than ever before. There's less "winging it" and more well-planned, educationally sound activities. Gone are the games that embarrassed a teenager for the sake of a youth group laugh. Replacing the Bible knowledge quizzes are active Bible studies that teach real-life applications. Even game times are frequently used to teach new faith insights. But one thing has remained relatively unchanged in youth ministry: discussions. Okay, two things: discussions and pizza.

Kids love to talk about what's happening in their world.

This book is designed to keep those discussions going in your group. *Controversial Discussion Starters* is a springboard into 34 hot discussions with your teenagers.

In Part One of this book, you'll find discussion starters in a familiar "debate" format. Using these discussion starters is as easy as one, two, three...four.

1. Photocopy the pages in this book for the question you want to discuss. Permission to photocopy these pages for one-time use by local churches is granted with the purchase of this

book. Also, photocopy the "Discussion Guidelines" handout on pages 10 to 11.

2. Form groups of no more than six to "argue" either side of the issue and give each group either a "yes" or a "no" position page. It's best if you have equal numbers of "yes" and "no" groups. And it's often most valuable for kids to be randomly assigned to a group. They'll learn a great deal about an issue if they have to argue it from a perspective they don't believe in. Give groups each a photocopy of the "Discussion Guidelines" handout.

3. Have teenagers each read the position statement on their handout, choose their role, explore the discussion starters and, most importantly, look up and read the related Bible passages. Also, have groups each read their photocopy of the "Discussion Guidelines" handout.

4. Match up "yes" and "no" groups and turn them loose to explore the issue. Be sure to have an adult sponsor available for each pair of "yes" and "no" groups. While it's important for kids to tackle the difficult issues and explore the Bible for answers, an adult sponsor can offer experience and maturity and guide kids toward a biblical understanding of the issue.

Plan on debriefing the discussions using the questions in the Closing the Discussion section of the "Discussion Guidelines" handout. Ask volunteers to tell what they learned through the discussion. Always have kids help you add closure to the issue by completing step four in the Closing the Discussion section of the "Discussion Guidelines" handout.

Part Two of this book gives you bonus activities to spark good discussions on hot topics. Some require a bit of preparation, others can be done on the spur of the moment. Each activity includes starter questions to get the discussion rolling. You may want to combine some of these activities with one of the discussion starters from Part One of the book.

However you use the discussion starters in this book, you're bound to open up a wide range of emotions in kids. Be sensitive to kids who have strong feelings about an issue. Don't be afraid to challenge kids who always say "it depends."

And always remember, your role isn't to tell kids what to believe—it's to help kids form Bible-based answers to difficult life issues.

Discussion Guidelines

Before the Discussion

(in your small group):

1. Choose roles for each of your group members from the following list:

- Spokesperson—opens in prayer, then leads the discussion for your group.
- Readers—look up and read aloud the Bible passages.
- Recorder—takes notes on your discussion strategies and planning.
- Taskmaster—keeps your group focused on the issues and reminds you to support your assigned position on the issue.
- Encouragers—encourage participation from all group members.

2. Read and discuss the position statement and discussion starters.

3. Explore the Bible passages. Both "yes" and "no" groups have the same list of scriptures, so familiarize yourself with all of them before deciding your strategy for the discussion. Have your readers read the passages and attempt to understand the context in which they were written. You may discover new insights in the scripture as you explore it more closely.

4. Plan how you'll approach the issue from the perspective you've been assigned. Your recorder should write down the ideas you have. You may not personally believe in this position, but for this discussion, you must do all you can to support the side you're on. Your taskmaster will remind you of this if necessary. You'll have an opportunity at the end of the discussion to share your personal feelings on the issue.

When you're ready to begin the discussion and have matched up with a group supporting the opposite position:

1. Have your spokespersons take turns opening in prayer, asking God's guidance in the discussion.

2. Decide how you'll proceed with the discussion:

● Informal style—Anyone can talk at any time.

● Debate style—Spokespersons take turns presenting their groups' position. Then groups alternate presenting their rebuttals.

3. Start your discussion . . . but always remember:

● Don't attack people personally; deal with the issue.

● Be polite.

● Support your side—even if you don't believe it.

● Try to uncover what the Bible says about the issue.

● Don't be afraid to challenge each other.

Closing the Discussion:

1. Take turns telling group members how you really feel about this issue.

2. Tell opposing group members specific things you appreciated about what they said and how they presented their position.

3. Take turns answering the following questions:

● How did you feel arguing this issue?

● What did you learn about the issue?

● How did the Bible passages help you find an answer to the issue?

● What aspects of the issue are still unclear to you?

4. Answer the following question with a statement everyone can agree with:

● Based on our discussion and the Bible passages we looked at, what can we say about this issue?

5. Form a group hug and close in prayer, asking God's continued guidance in dealing with this issue.

Part One:

Discussion
Starters

Faith Issues

● Can you believe in New Age philosophies and be a Christian?

● Is regular church attendance necessary for all Christians?

● Will people who believe in non-Christian religions such as Buddhism, Hinduism and Islam go to heaven?

● Does the Bible require Christians to tell others about their faith?

● Is it okay for Christians to use illegal means to protest issues they strongly believe in?

● Should Bible clubs be allowed to meet on public school property?

Yes

YES Position Statement:

The teachings of the New Age movement don't go against Christianity, so there's no reason for the two to be in opposition. New Agers aren't anti-Christ, they're just wary of the exclusive club called Christianity.

New Agers are often more accepting of people than Christians. And many New Agers have lots of good things to say about Jesus. The New Age movement certainly has made a difference in the world: helping people feel good about themselves, promoting unity among all people and cleaning up the environment.

Besides, as Christians, we're supposed to seek the truth. Maybe there's some truth in the New Age philosophies that we're missing.

YES Discussion Starters:

- What's wrong with expanding your horizons and learning from other faiths?
- New Age philosophies support Jesus as a great teacher.
- The New Age movement has done a lot of good for our world— especially in the area of environmental concerns.
- How can we as Christians be so bold to assume our way is the only way?
- New Age beliefs can't hurt you.
- You can love God and discover truths from other sources, too.
- New Agers are simply enlightened Christians.

Bible Passages:

- Matthew 24:3-14
- Romans 16:17-19
- Galatians 1:6-9
- Proverbs 8:10-11
- Proverbs 10:14
- Colossians 2:6-15
- Isaiah 8:19-20
- Proverbs 4:5-8
- 1 Timothy 6:20-21

No

NO Position Statement:

No other gods should be placed before the one true God. Since New Age philosophy promotes the idea that each person is a "god," it's an anti-Christian philosophy. And just because many New Agers do good things doesn't make their beliefs biblical.

By opening up their faith to the teachings of the New Age movement, Christians open the door for Satan to sneak in. Many New Agers believe you can gain wisdom from *any* religious source, including Satanism. For this reason, New Age philosophy isn't compatible with Christianity.

NO Discussion Starters:

● How can you reconcile acceptance of New Age philosophies with the Bible's warning about false teachers?

● New Age philosophies don't recognize Jesus as the only way to God.

● The New Age movement actually undermines the Christian faith by minimizing the importance of Jesus.

● The New Age movement preaches that people can reach heaven without God. The Bible says Jesus is the only way (John 14:6).

● To believe in New Age philosophies, you have to dilute your Christian faith.

Bible Passages:

● Matthew 24:3-14
● Romans 16:17-19
● Galatians 1:6-9
● Proverbs 8:10-11
● Proverbs 10:14

● Colossians 2:6-15
● Isaiah 8:19-20
● Proverbs 4:5-8
● 1 Timothy 6:20-21

YES Position Statement:

Yes

Going to church may seem like a waste of time on occasion, but it's critical to spiritual development. Without the regular challenge offered by the pastor or the learning gained from Sunday school, Christians can easily be distracted from their faith.

And no, you can't get the same spiritual food at home—unless you start a church in your home, that is. If you were invited to a friend's house for dinner, you wouldn't say, "No thanks, but drop the food by here anyway" would you? No. That's because the fellowship is just as important as the food. It's the same with church.

YES Discussion Starters:

- Church gives you a place to grow in faith.
- How can you learn about Christ without church?
- Why would Christ set up the basis for the church if he didn't intend for us to be faithful to it?
- Without church, Christianity would weaken and fall.
- If you don't attend church, you're more likely to fall away from Christ.
- Paul called the church the body of Christ. So for you to say you don't need the church to survive as a Christian is the same as a hand saying it doesn't need the rest of the body to survive.

Bible Passages:

- Acts 2:36-47
- 1 Corinthians 12:12-27
- Ephesians 1:21-23
- Ephesians 5:25-27
- Psalm 100:1-5
- Exodus 20:8-11
- Hebrews 10:19-39

NO Position Statement:

No

Sunday church today is just an audience gathering in a building. There's nothing "magical" about meeting on Sunday mornings. In the early days of Christianity, there were no church buildings. People met in each other's homes to pray and worship. You don't have to go to church regularly to maintain your Christian faith. As long as you have close Christian relationships, you'll be okay. In fact, you're probably better off than people who just go to church once or twice a week.

Besides, if you look around at the state of the church today, you'll discover more dysfunctional churches than healthy ones. What benefit do Christians get if they attend a church that's misusing or misdirecting its members?

The true church is formed out of individuals and the relationships they build with other Christians. That can happen in a church building—or in a shopping mall.

NO Discussion Starters:

- You don't need a building with a steeple to be a Christian.
- Today's church is corrupt, controlling and dysfunctional.
- Why do you need to attend boring church services to grow in faith?
- The church has become too political and too impersonal.
- Attending church doesn't guarantee you'll grow in faith.
- The Bible teaches that Christians are justified by faith in Jesus alone. That means we don't have to "jump through any hoops," such as going to church regularly, in order to be accepted by God.

Bible Passages:

- Acts 2:36-47
- 1 Corinthians 12:12-27
- Ephesians 1:21-23
- Ephesians 5:26-27
- Psalm 100:1-5
- Exodus 20:8-11
- Hebrews 10:19-39

WILL PEOPLE WHO BELIEVE IN NON-CHRISTIAN RELIGIONS SUCH AS BUDDHISM, HINDUISM AND ISLAM GO TO HEAVEN?

YES Position Statement:

Yes

There's only one God. It's only logical that the major world religions worship the same God Christians worship. They just do it in a different way. Even the Bible acknowledges that God is unfathomable. Perhaps one of the mysteries of God is that he's big enough to be God in different ways to different people.

And we know from the Bible that God is a merciful God. What kind of God would send millions of faithful followers in the Buddhist, Hindu or Moslem traditions to hell?

Although no human can truly know the mind of God, there's no reason to think true believers of other faiths won't meet us in heaven.

YES Discussion Starters:

● All major religions worship the same God.

● Could a merciful God send millions of well-intentioned people to hell?

● For Christians, Jesus is the only way, but that doesn't mean there aren't other ways to get to heaven.

● We can't fully understand God's mysterious ways.

● Perhaps there are different heavens for different religions.

● The Bible is just one of God's holy books. Other religious books tell of different ways to heaven.

Bible Passages:

● 1 Timothy 4:1-16
● John 14:6
● John 15:1-4
● Acts 4:12

● Revelation 10:7
● Job 11:7-9
● John 3:16
● Matthew 28:19

NO Position Statement:

The only way to heaven is through Jesus Christ.

Because the Bible leaves no space for other interpretations, the opening sentence is all you need to support this position. Though it may sound presumptuous or boastful to other religions, there's no question that God has chosen Christians to be his people.

If you assume the Bible is God's Word—however you might interpret it—you can't deny the message that there's only one way to heaven.

As for the other major world religions, Jesus commanded his followers (that means us) to preach the good news of salvation through Christ to them, too. If there were other ways to heaven, why would Jesus give such a command?

NO Discussion Starters:

- The Bible clearly says the only way to God is through Jesus.
- Other faiths have misinterpreted history and don't worship the same God.
- God is a loving God, but he has made it clear only Christians will go to heaven.
- Why would God commission his followers to preach in the whole world if other faiths were just as good as Christianity?
- To live as Christians, we must believe the only way to God is through Christ.

Bible Passages:

- 1 Timothy 4:1-16
- John 14:6
- John 15:1-4
- Acts 4:12
- Revelation 10:7
- Job 11:7-9
- John 3:16
- Matthew 28:19

Yes

YES Position Statement:

Christ commanded his followers to preach to and teach all the nations about God's gift of eternal life. And that command is still valid today.

While it's certainly "fashionable" to let people believe what they want, this perspective isn't biblical. It is clearly God's will for Christians to reach out whenever we can to tell others about God's love. And while that doesn't mean each Christian has to go to seminary, it does mean we need to be ready to share our faith.

It's a weak excuse to say that faith is a personal thing. Of course faith is personal, but when you discover the wonderful power of God's love, you have to share it with someone.

YES Discussion Starters:

● The Great Commission tells all Christians to share their faith.

● How can you be a true Christian if you never let anyone know about it?

● A silent faith is almost as useless as no faith at all.

● If we don't share our faith with others, we're disobeying God.

● How will the world know about Christ if we don't share our faith?

● If you're a Christian but don't let others know, you're a hypocrite.

Bible Passages:

● 2 Timothy 1:3-14
● Acts 8:25
● Colossians 4:5-6
● Ephesians 4:11-13
● 2 Corinthians 4:3-12
● Matthew 28:18-20
● Luke 8:16-18
● Mark 4:11-12

20

NO Position Statement:

The Bible describes in great detail how each person has a different role in the body of Christ. Some are preachers, some are teachers and others may be encouragers of the faith. But the key to understanding those roles is the word "some." Not everyone is cut out to tell others about God's love.

Christ died to save all kinds of people, including people who are great speakers and people who can't begin to put a sentence together with any chance of being understood. Some Christians share their faith simply by their example. They don't have to say a single word. Actions speak louder than words.

It's like the song says, "They'll know we are Christians by our love."

No Discussion Starters:

● Not every person is good at sharing his or her faith.

● The most important thing about being a Christian is that you love God. That doesn't mean you have to tell other people.

● Some people are given the gift of speaking, but others aren't.

● If you follow God, people will know you're a Christian by your actions.

● Some people will stop listening if you try to tell them about Christ.

Bible Passages:

● 2 Timothy 1:3-14
● Acts 8:25
● Colossians 4:5-6
● Ephesians 4:11-13
● 2 Corinthians 4:3-12
● Matthew 28:18-20
● Luke 8:16-18
● Mark 4:11-12

IS IT OKAY FOR CHRISTIANS TO USE ILLEGAL MEANS TO PROTEST ISSUES THEY STRONGLY BELIEVE IN?

YES Position Statement:

Yes

The real question with this issue is: Does the end ever justify the means?

The answer is...yes. If the goal is to bring Christ to all the world, Christians may sometimes have to break the world's rules. For example, if Christians hadn't (illegally) smuggled Bibles into Iron Curtain countries, many people probably wouldn't be Christians today. Sometimes a powerful action is needed to get people's attention on an important faith issue. If that action draws attention to the real issue, it doesn't matter how you get the impact. It's best if no one is hurt by the action. But both martyrs and violent revolutionists have brought positive change to the world.

YES Discussion Starters:

● If the world's rules prevent you from speaking out, the rules must be broken to preach God's will.

● As long as no one's hurt, you can do anything to get your message across.

● Sometimes you need to break the rules to get people's attention.

● God's rules supersede any earthly rules.

● Everyone else breaks the rules, so why can't Christians?

Bible Passages:

● Matthew 23:1-12
● Romans 13:1-5
● Galatians 5:16-18
● John 18:36
● Ephesians 4:31-32

● Colossians 3:1-11
● Leviticus 19:11-12
● 1 Peter 2:13-17
● 1 Peter 3:13-16

22

NO Position Statement:

It's too easy to use the excuse that "the end justifies the means." There are always alternative routes to bringing about change in the world. And too often, Christians charge ahead with "holy" reasons for doing illegal things. Doing illegal things to get a point across usually gets the wrong point across: that Christians do illegal things.

The Bible charges Christians to respect authority. That includes respecting the laws we've been given. This doesn't mean Christians can't speak out, but they must stay within the boundaries of the law.

Christians need to set a good example for the world by following the law.

NO Discussion Starters:

- God wants us to follow the rules and laws of our governments.
- There are always legal ways to make your point.
- Through prayer and perseverance, all things are possible.
- It's hypocritical to break the law to make a point about Christian faith.
- What kind of example does a Christian who breaks the law show to non-Christians?

Bible Passages:

- Matthew 23:1-12
- Romans 13:1-5
- Galatians 5:16-18
- John 18:36
- Ephesians 4:31-32
- Colossians 3:1-11
- Leviticus 19:11-12
- 1 Peter 2:13-17
- 1 Peter 3:13-16

23

YES Position Statement:

Two significant goals can be accomplished by allowing Christians to meet on public school grounds: First, young Christians can grow in faith through the regular support and fellowship that meeting together brings. And second, clubs become a non-threatening way for Christians to invite non-Christian friends to explore the meaning of a Christian faith.

If other groups want to meet on public school property, that's fine. The value gained by Christians meeting together in prayer and worship will far outweigh the turmoil caused by other non-Christian groups meeting at school.

Our country was founded on freedom of religious expression, and that freedom should also be available in our public schools.

YES Discussion Starters:

● Christians should have the opportunity to meet in any location they desire.

● The government shouldn't be able to prevent freedom of religious expression in public schools.

● Without the influence of Christianity in public schools, the values in society will deteriorate.

● No one forces people to join Bible clubs, so what's so terrible about them?

Bible Passages:

● Matthew 22:21
● Matthew 16:19-20
● Galatians 5:18
● 1 Peter 2:13-17
● 1 Peter 3:13-16
● Jude 17-23
● Hebrews 10:24-25

NO Position Statement:

The church was created to allow Christians to meet regularly to learn about their faith and enjoy fellowship. Public schools were created for a different purpose—to educate people. There's no reason to have Christian clubs meet on school property when the same need is being met at church.

Additionally, if Christian clubs are allowed to meet at public schools, all kinds of clubs must be allowed to meet. That could include anything from white supremacy clubs to Satanism clubs.

Christians can support each other in many different ways. They don't need to cause division in their communities by challenging the issue of separation of church and state.

NO Discussion Starters:

● If a Bible club can meet at a public school, so can any other kind of club.
● Religion and education shouldn't be mixed.
● Bible clubs don't help others get to know Jesus any more effectively than the church does.
● Bible clubs are usually exclusive cliques.
● Kids can meet on their own, anyway, so why do they need a special meeting place at a public school?

Bible Passages:

● Matthew 22:21
● Matthew 16:19-20
● Galatians 5:18
● 1 Peter 2:13-17

● 1 Peter 3:13-16
● Jude 17-23
● Hebrews 10:24-25

Health Issues

● Is it wrong to take steroids or other body-altering drugs?

● Would drug problems diminish if marijuana were legalized?

● Is it okay for Christians to drink alcoholic beverages socially?

Yes

YES Position Statement:

All body- or mind-altering drugs are dangerous. That includes drugs such as anabolic steroids. While it may seem that steroids are simply a shortcut to a stronger body, the known side effects clearly point out that steroids are just a shortcut to a less productive life—or even death.

Besides the obvious dangers of steroids, the truth is there's no reason to sidestep the work it takes to look your best. The discipline it takes to build a better body is a healthy thing that's missed when people take shortcuts. Shortcuts like that never pay off in the long run.

YES Discussion Starters:

- Steroids can do great damage to your body.
- Why would someone want to hurt his or her body to look good?
- What's important is on the inside—not the outside.
- Is it worth risking your life to have a better body?
- Steroids are a dangerous shortcut.
- If you work out without drugs, you feel better about yourself.
- Good health is more important than good looks.

Bible Passages:

- 1 Samuel 16:1-13
- Romans 7:14-25
- Romans 12:1-2
- Romans 13:11-14
- 1 Corinthians 6:19-20
- Matthew 20:25-27
- 1 Kings 2:1-4
- Ecclesiastes 1:1-18

28

IS IT WRONG TO TAKE STEROIDS OR OTHER BODY-ALTERING DRUGS?

NO Position Statement:

No

Taking a drug to experience a "high" is different from taking a drug to help you gain more muscles or a better-looking body. When you take steroids, you simply enhance the work you're already doing to be stronger and more muscular.

Steroids can also enhance a person's self-esteem by helping that person see how strong and good-looking he or she can be. Besides, to compete in today's athletics, steroids are a must.

If you carefully monitor the risks you're taking, there's nothing wrong with taking steroids.

NO Discussion Starters:

- Steroids can't hurt you if you know what you're doing.
- What's wrong with improving your looks or your abilities?
- The Bible wants us to do our best in everything, and steroids help us do that.
- To compete in athletics, you have to take steroids.
- Steroids and other body-enhancers only help you reach your potential faster.

Bible Passages:

- 1 Samuel 16:1-13
- Romans 7:14-25
- Romans 12:1-2
- Romans 13:11-14
- 1 Corinthians 6:19-20
- Matthew 20:25-27
- 1 Kings 2:1-4
- Ecclesiastes 1:1-18

Yes

YES Position Statement:

People naturally crave what they can't have. Often people will do things simply because they're forbidden or there's some kind of mystery attached to the action. That's exactly why marijuana holds such an attraction, especially to kids, who naturally want to challenge authority. But if the mystery and challenge to authority were gone, kids wouldn't have a reason to try the drugs.

While the drug problem wouldn't completely disappear, it would diminish because government control would keep the drug safe. And the availability of the drug would substantially reduce the dangerous crime element from being involved in selling the drug.

Legalizing marijuana doesn't mean you have to try it. But it will make trying it less appealing, especially to kids.

YES Discussion Starters:

● If the drug were easy to get, there would be no challenge or risk, and so people wouldn't want it.

● Legalizing the drug could give the government more control on safety issues.

● In countries where marijuana is legal, there are fewer drug problems.

● Most people say marijuana isn't harmful.

● Everyone tries it anyway, so why not just make it legal?

Bible Passages:

● Romans 8:5-17
● Romans 14:13-18
● 1 Corinthians 6:12
● 1 Thessalonians 4:4

● Ecclesiastes 3:1-8
● Titus 3:1-7
● Ecclesiastes 7:15-17

No

NO Position Statement:

The Bible warns us not to be taken in by the passions of the world. And the only reason for smoking marijuana is for the feeling—the passion—it provides.

The instant marijuana is legalized, millions of people will try it to see what it's like. Kids and adults will revel in the government's "approval" of the drug. And instead of lessening the interest in the drug, people will become more attracted to it. People who otherwise would never have the opportunity to use the drug will suddenly have access to it.

To legalize marijuana is to say "there's nothing wrong with drugs" to the kids of the United States.

NO Discussion Starters:

● Making a drug legal won't change the dangerous effects the drug has.

● New drugs will replace the popularity of marijuana.

● Legalizing "pot" will make it available to more people who otherwise wouldn't have tried it.

● Legalizing one drug could lead to a trend of legalizing all drugs.

● Making a dangerous drug readily available will not make it less appealing.

Bible Passages:

● Romans 8:5-17
● Romans 14:13-18
● 1 Corinthians 6:12
● 1 Thessalonians 4:4

● Ecclesiastes 3:1-8
● Titus 3:1-7
● Ecclesiastes 7:15-17

YES Position Statement:

There's nothing in the Bible that says drinking alcoholic beverages is a sin. In fact, most of the people in Jesus' time drank wine regularly. Jesus' first miracle changed water into wine. The only issue about drinking that the Bible condemns is drunkenness.

In social settings where alcohol is served, Christians should be free to have a drink if they enjoy doing so. Christians who claim the Bible says it's wrong to drink don't uplift Christ. Instead, they uplift their "holier than thou" attitude, which turns non-Christians off to the gospel. But a Christian who isn't shy to say he or she likes a glass of wine once in a while can sit with the "sinners" without scaring them off.

Responsible drinking isn't a sin. It's a viable option for all Christians.

YES Discussion Starters:

- People drank wine in Bible times, and it was never condemned by God's law.
- As long as you drink responsibly, it's okay to drink.
- There is no place in the Bible where it specifically says drinking is wrong.
- In moderation, alcohol can actually be good for you.
- Drinking with friends is a great way to socialize.
- Jesus actively supported other people's drinking by turning water into wine.

Bible Passages:

- Psalm 104:15
- Proverbs 20:1
- Proverbs 23:20
- John 2:3-10
- Romans 13:11-13
- Ephesians 5:18
- 1 Timothy 5:23

NO Position Statement:

The only reason people drink alcoholic beverages is because drinking makes them feel good. Some claim it's because they like the taste. But if that's the case, why don't those people simply drink non-alcoholic wine and beer? Doing something because it feels good is a dangerous habit to get into. That's how people become drug addicts, sex addicts or alcoholics.

The Bible warns Christians not to do anything that may make another Christian "stumble." And to many Christians, drinking is wrong. A Christian who drinks in a social setting may wrongly influence another Christian or cause that other Christian to lose faith. No one needs alcohol to live a fulfilled life. And Christians need it even less.

NO Discussion Starters:

- Alcohol impairs your judgment.
- The Bible warns against drunkenness.
- By drinking in social settings, you could wrongly influence another Christian.
- It's dangerous to toy with alcohol since it can be addictive.
- Drinking alcohol is illegal for teenagers anyway.
- Non-Christians may question your faith.

Bible Passages:

- Psalm 104:15
- Proverbs 20:1
- Proverbs 23:20
- John 2:3-10
- Romans 13:11-13
- Ephesians 5:18
- 1 Timothy 5:23

Media Issues

● Is it okay to watch R-rated movies without parental permission?

● Is it wrong for Christians to watch or listen to raunchy comedians?

● Do extreme music styles (such as death metal) have a negative impact on listeners' lives?

YES Position Statement:

Yes

Parents don't need to know everything their kids do. If they did, they couldn't handle it anyway. Today's R-rated movies are no big deal. Most of the language is no worse than what kids hear at school. The violence isn't any more real than the violence you read about every day in the newspaper. And the sex and nudity can't really hurt you.

Besides, some of the best films are rated R. Responsible teenagers can make good choices on their own about what movies to watch. And as long as they evaluate each film appropriately, there's no reason to run to Mom and Dad to get advice about something they probably know little about.

YES Discussion Starters:

● Teenagers are capable of making up their own minds about whether they should watch an R-rated movie.
● Parents don't need to know everything their kids do.
● R-rated movies can't hurt you.
● Some of the best movies are rated R.
● Parents don't care if you see R-rated movies.
● Some R-rated movies have significant themes or positive messages.

Bible Passages:

● Psalm 139:1-24
● Exodus 20:12
● Proverbs 11:3
● Ephesians 4:17-19
● Romans 15:1
● Proverbs 12:21

NO Position Statement:

No

Movies are rated R for excessive violence, sex, nudity and bad language. The Bible tells Christians to steer clear of such things.

It may be true that some R-rated movies have solid lessons in them. And it may be true that watching those movies doesn't have to be a negative experience. But to sneak around your parents to watch an R-rated movie is wrong.

The Bible doesn't mention movies, but it does mention parents. It says to honor and obey your parents. Is it honorable to hide the fact that you watched an R-rated movie at a friend's house last night? No.

The teenager who gets a parent's permission before watching an R-rated film also builds a foundation of trust with his or her parent.

NO Discussion Starters:

● While some R-rated movies might have a positive message, parents should always be a part of the decision to watch them.

● Most R-rated movies have gratuitous violence and sex in them.

● It's wrong to hide questionable actions from parents.

● Younger teenagers shouldn't see R-rated films without a parent's or guardian's permission at all, according to the definition of the rating.

● The best relationship to have with parents is one that's open and honest.

Bible Passages:

● Psalm 139:1-24
● Exodus 20:12
● Proverbs 11:3
● Ephesians 4:17-19
● Romans 15:1
● Proverbs 12:21

Yes

YES Position Statement:

Garbage in, garbage out.

It's an old saying but a very biblical one. The gross sex jokes and bad language that come out of many comedians' mouths aren't worth the time it takes to listen. Paul warns Christians not to fill our minds with bad things, such as raunchy humor.

Sure—people laugh at raunchy humor. That's because it shocks people and makes them nervous, not because it's funny. There's nothing wrong with humor because we all need to laugh. But raunchy humor makes people feel guilty and dirty.

YES Discussion Starters:

● Christians should avoid all negative things.

● Listening to bad language is unhealthy.

● Raunchy humor makes you laugh because you're uncomfortable or shocked, not because the person is funny.

● The Bible warns us to think on only good things.

● If we watch or listen to raunchy comedians, we encourage them to continue.

● What's so funny about swearing and sex jokes?

Bible Passages:

● Psalm 139:1-24
● Ephesians 4:8
● 1 John 2:15
● Psalm 109:16-20
● Romans 3:9-20
● James 3:1-12
● Proverbs 12:21

IS IT WRONG FOR CHRISTIANS TO WATCH OR LISTEN TO RAUNCHY COMEDIANS?

NO Position Statement:

Laughter is good medicine. And whatever gets people to laugh is okay (as long as no one is hurt). Bad humor is harmless.

Christians don't have to hide their heads in the sand every time someone says a bad word or tells an off-color joke. Christians need to lighten up and enjoy laughing, too.

As long as Christians have the same basic traits as the rest of humanity, they're going to laugh at the same kinds of things. And that's okay.

NO Discussion Starters:

- Words can't really hurt you.
- Not all the jokes are dirty.
- It isn't wrong to listen to raunchy humor in private.
- There isn't much clean humor left.
- Dirty jokes make people laugh, and laughter is good for people.

Bible Passages:

- Psalm 139:1-24
- Ephesians 4:8
- 1 John 2:15
- Psalm 109:16-20
- Romans 3:9-20
- James 3:1-12
- Proverbs 12:21

DO EXTREME MUSIC STYLES (SUCH AS DEATH METAL) HAVE A NEGATIVE IMPACT ON LISTENERS' LIVES?

YES Position Statement:

How does church music make you feel? heavy metal? jazz? dance? classical? If you thought of a feeling word such as "bored," "angry" or "excited," you've proven the point of this position.

The music we listen to does affect us. When you add depressing lyrics to otherwise depressing music, you're bound to feel, well...depressed. And extreme music styles typically sing the praises of death, worthlessness or anarchy. Feed yourself enough of these sentiments and you're bound to be affected by them.

Music worth listening to should either challenge us or encourage us, not scare us to death.

YES Discussion Starters:

- Negative music promotes negative attitudes.
- Most fans of death metal are always depressed.
- There's no hope or joy in negative music.
- The messages of most extreme music styles are depressing, sick or morbid.
- Music should lift people up and make them happy.

Bible Passages:

- 1 Samuel 16:14-23
- 2 Samuel 6:5
- Isaiah 5:11-12
- John 15:19
- Proverbs 11:20
- Jeremiah 17:10
- Lamentations 1-5

DO EXTREME MUSIC STYLES (SUCH AS DEATH METAL) HAVE A NEGATIVE IMPACT ON LISTENERS' LIVES?

NO Position Statement:

Music is entertainment. Most people who listen to extreme music styles such as industrial music or death metal choose to do so just because it "sounds good." And many don't even listen to the lyrics.

If music really had the power to affect people, country fans would be sleeping with other people's wives, blues fans would be standing in line to commit suicide, alternative fans would be doing away with all the politicians, and rap fans would be taking over the world. Music is just music.

NO Discussion Starters:

- Most people don't listen to the lyrics.
- Extreme music is just a form of escape or entertainment.
- Music can't hurt you any more than bad language can hurt you.
- Some of the messages in the songs are actually positive.
- Listening to extreme music helps people express their feelings rather than bottle them in.

Bible Passages:

- 1 Samuel 16:14-23
- 2 Samuel 6:5
- Isaiah 5:11-12
- John 15:19
- Proverbs 11:20
- Jeremiah 17:10
- Lamentations 1-5

41

Relationship Issues

● If a friend confides in you about his or her drinking problem, should you tell someone without his or her permission?

● Is it okay for Christians to date non-Christians?

● Is it ever best to withold the truth from parents?

● If you discovered your brother or sister taking drugs, should you tell your parents?

● Is it ever okay to use bad language?

IF A FRIEND CONFIDES IN YOU ABOUT HIS OR HER DRINKING PROBLEM, SHOULD YOU TELL SOMEONE WITHOUT HIS OR HER PERMISSION?

YES Position Statement:

Yes

A hidden drinking problem is still a drinking problem. And friends should be strong enough to say so.

If you try to find help for your friend, you could make a difference. Then, instead of reading in the morning paper about the drunk teenager who ran head on into a church van, you might read about the teenager who turned his or her life around.

The risk of losing a friendship is worth the chance of saving someone's life.

YES Discussion Starters:

- If you don't tell someone, your friend might hurt him- or herself.
- It's a friend's responsibility to look out for a friend.
- Sometimes the most important things to do are the hardest.
- It's better to risk losing a friend than to have a friend risk losing his or her life.
- Alcoholism is a serious problem, and alcoholics need help.
- If a friend confides in you, perhaps he or she is really crying for help.

Bible Passages:

- Proverbs 18:24
- Proverbs 27:9
- Proverbs 27:17
- John 15:13
- Leviticus 19:11-12
- Micah 7:5
- Proverbs 11:13
- Proverbs 12:18

44

NO Position Statement:

Nothing you do will change your friend's mind about his or her drinking problem. Alcoholics have to decide for themselves whether or not to get help.

The only thing you do when you tell on a friend is risk losing that friendship. And with your friend in trouble, he or she needs you to stay faithful.

It's best not to risk the friendship by telling other people about your friend's problem. It's better to stay quiet and let your friend know you'll be there when he or she is ready to ask for help.

NO Discussion Starters:

● Friends don't betray each other's confidence.

● Telling someone about a friend's drinking problem won't necessarily help the friend overcome the problem.

● If you've confronted your friend, that's all you can do.

● Your friend will have to decide for him- or herself to get help.

● Your friend trusted you to keep the information quiet.

Bible Passages:

● Proverbs 18:24
● Proverbs 27:9
● Proverbs 27:17
● John 15:13
● Leviticus 19:11-12
● Micah 7:5
● Proverbs 11:13
● Proverbs 12:18

YES Position Statement:

Christians should be able to date whoever they want. There are plenty of good people in the world who aren't Christians. Some non-Christians probably have more good qualities than some Christians.

And if dating is simply a way to get to know someone of the opposite sex, what's wrong with getting to know a non-Christian? It's not like you're committing to marrying that person or anything. Besides, you might be able to lead him or her to Christ.

YES Discussion Starters:

- Just because you date someone doesn't mean you'll actually marry him or her.
- Love can overcome all obstacles—even differences in religious beliefs.
- You can always share your faith with the person.
- If you have a strong faith, you can handle the differences.
- If you could only date Christians, your choices would be limited.
- As long as you date a "good" person, it's okay.

Bible Passages:

- 2 Corinthians 7:8-16
- Hosea 1:2-9
- Malachi 2:15-16
- Matthew 19:1-12
- 2 Corinthians 6:14-17
- 1 Corinthians 13:1-13
- Mark 16:15

IS IT OKAY FOR CHRISTIANS TO DATE NON-CHRISTIANS?

NO Position Statement:

A Christian who dates a non-Christian is taking a risk. He or she risks a difficult decision in the future by investing love in someone who wouldn't be the best mate in the long-run. In addition, a Christian must often compromise his or her faith to accommodate the non-Christian's beliefs.

There's nothing wrong with Christians associating with non-Christians. But love is a powerful thing, and dating a non-Christian could too easily turn into a difficult situation. It's just too easy for a Christian to fall in love with a non-Christian and then say, "I can change him (or her) after we're married."

Dating a non-Christian is kind of like jumping off a cliff. It can feel good at first, but you can't avoid the crash at the end. It's not worth the risk.

NO Discussion Starters:

● If you date someone who isn't a Christian, your own faith could falter.

● If you date a non-Christian, you might fall in love and want to marry him or her.

● Non-Christians don't have the same value system as Christians.

● You can't count on converting someone you care for.

● People should date people with similar beliefs and values.

● A Christian couple should always put Christ first, but a couple where one person isn't a Christian can't do that.

Bible Passages:

● 2 Corinthians 7:8-16
● Hosea 1:2-9
● Malachi 2:15-16
● Matthew 19:1-12

● 2 Corinthians 6:14-17
● 1 Corinthians 13:1-13
● Mark 16:15

YES Position Statement:

Yes

There's nothing wrong with hiding things from parents that they wouldn't understand anyway.

If you discovered you were going to flunk a class at school but then later found a way to bring your grade up, what benefit would you have gained by getting your parents upset at your potential flunking grade? None.

Hiding the truth may actually improve your relationship with your parents since they won't have to process and deal with all the things that might cause them to worry or get upset. As long as the important things are communicated, withholding the truth from time to time can't hurt—and can actually help keep the peace.

YES Discussion Starters:

- Parents don't have to know everything you do.
- Parents don't care about everything you do anyway.
- Little lies won't harm your relationship with your parents.
- Parents don't always understand, so sometimes it's important to keep things to yourself.
- If parents knew all the things their teenagers did, they'd go crazy.
- Choosing not to share something with someone isn't the same as lying.

Bible Passages:

- Exodus 2:1-10
- Luke 2:41-50
- Ecclesiastes 12:14
- Ephesians 6:1-2
- Proverbs 6:16-19
- Genesis 27:1-46

NO Position Statement:

Trust is built on honesty and respect. And teenagers who withhold the truth do nothing but break down trust in their families.

The pattern is set when a teenager hides one little problem or lack of judgment from his or her parents. Then the lying becomes easier and, eventually, it becomes a nasty habit.

The Bible teaches that Christians should be honest. Not honest sometimes. Not honest about most things. Just honest. Period.

The place to start is at home.

NO Discussion Starters:

- You can't develop trust with your parents if you lie to them.
- Parents deserve to know what's going on with their children.
- Lying is always wrong.
- Parents often have wise answers to difficult or embarrassing problems.
- Parents respect children who come to them with tough situations.
- If you love your parents, you'll be honest with them.

Bible Passages:

- Exodus 2:1-10
- Luke 2:41-50
- Ecclesiastes 12:14
- Ephesians 6:1-2
- Proverbs 6:16-19
- Genesis 27:1-46

IF YOU DISCOVERED YOUR BROTHER OR SISTER WAS TAKING DRUGS, SHOULD YOU TELL YOUR PARENTS?

Yes

YES Position Statement:

The worst thing you could do in this situation is hide such a serious problem out of respect or love for your sibling. The truth is that reporting your sibling's problem to someone is the most loving thing you can do for him or her.

No matter what kind of relationship you have with your sibling, you can't risk letting your brother or sister waste away just because your relationship might turn negative. It's best to confront the sibling first, then go right to your parents to get the situation out in the open.

Taking drugs is no game. If the problem remains hidden, so do the potentially life-threatening effects of the drugs.

YES Discussion Starters:

● Parents have a right to know what's going on in the family.
● It's better to confront a problem than to hide it.
● Siblings will eventually forgive you if you tell.
● The risk of being disliked by a family member is worth bringing the issue into the open.
● Your brother or sister can't get help until someone identifies there's a problem.
● Drug addiction is not something your sibling can get out of by him- or herself.

Bible Passages:

● Proverbs 18:24
● Genesis 13:8
● Psalm 133:1-3
● John 15:13
● Leviticus 19:11-12
● 1 Corinthians 6:9-10
● 1 Peter 3:8
● Proverbs 11:13

50

IF YOU DISCOVERED YOUR BROTHER OR SISTER WAS TAKING DRUGS, SHOULD YOU TELL YOUR PARENTS?

No

NO Position Statement:

If a sibling is taking drugs, he or she has to take ownership of the problem. You can't rescue him or her. And you'll only start a big fight by "snitching" on him or her.

Confront your brother or sister if you think that will make a difference. But most kids won't listen anyway. If your sibling is like most teenagers, he or she will experiment with drugs for a while, then never do them again.

Don't risk breaking your family apart over something that may go away in a few weeks.

NO Discussion Starters:

● What your siblings do is none of your business.
● You can't be responsible for your sibling's actions.
● Parents won't understand your sibling's natural desire to experiment with drugs.
● It's wrong to break trust with your brother or sister.
● You can't do anything to help your sibling until he or she thinks there's a problem.

Bible Passages:

● Proverbs 18:24
● Genesis 13:8
● Psalm 133:1-3
● John 15:13

● Leviticus 19:11-12
● 1 Corinthians 6:9-10
● 1 Peter 3:8
● Proverbs 11:13

51

YES Position Statement:

Yes

An occasional swear word won't send you to hell. And as long as you don't use God's name inappropriately, you won't be doing anything that goes against the Bible. Bad language probably isn't appropriate in church or during class at school. But it's fine for Christians to spit out a bad word or two when something goes wrong or when that hammer misses the nail and hits the finger.

Bad language is a part of our society and it's difficult to avoid. So, rather than stifle the natural expression that wants to come out, Christians should be honest and say a bad word once in a while.

It's a great way to release frustration.

YES Discussion Starters:

- Words are just words.
- Swearing is okay as long as you don't take the Lord's name in vain.
- Swear words are good ways to release frustration.
- What you say in private doesn't offend anyone.
- Bad language is an accepted part of society.
- Christians come across as fake if they don't say a bad word now and then.

Bible Passages:

- Deuteronomy 5:11
- Psalm 44:21
- Proverbs 20:20
- Matthew 9:10-12
- Romans 2:15-16
- Ephesians 5:4
- Colossians 3:8
- James 3:1-12

NO Position Statement:

No

The words you use are a reflection of your character and your beliefs. Swear words are not the kind of words Christians should use.

Although the world has determined that swear words are an everyday option, Christians can choose to go against the world. Christians also need to heed the warning in the Bible against using God's name in vain or cursing other people.

NO Discussion Starters:

- Godliness is not optional for Christians.
- Swearing makes people look stupid.
- People can control the words they speak.
- The Bible tells us not to take the Lord's name in vain.
- Other Christians might lose faith because of a fellow Christian's foul mouth.
- Christians are to set an example for the world in all things—including speech.

Bible Passages:

- Deuteronomy 5:11
- Psalm 44:21
- Proverbs 20:20
- Matthew 9:10-12
- Romans 2:15-16
- Ephesians 5:4
- Colossians 3:8
- James 3:1-12

School Issues

● Is cheating ever okay?

● Is the experience of going to school more important than getting good grades?

● Is it best to take a year off from school before going to college?

● Is the prospect of making more money the best reason to further your education?

Yes

YES Position Statement:

Most people cheat because they really need to, not to make themselves look smarter than they really are. And if that's all people use cheating for, there's little harm in it. People who cheat often gain the benefit of the grade they could've gotten anyway, but they just didn't have time to study like their classmates. Life is hard for some teenagers, such as those who have jobs or children to raise. They shouldn't be penalized with a bad grade just because they don't have time to study like other kids. After all, they're smart people, so why shouldn't they get a good grade?

YES Discussion Starters:

● Cheating isn't cheating if it's used to help someone get out of a tight spot.

● Everyone cheats sometime.

● If you know you could learn it, why waste the time studying just to prove it to a teacher?

● What's wrong with cheating on a test that will never matter to you again in life?

Bible Passages:

● Malachi 1:12-14
● Genesis 27:1-41
● 1 Samuel 12:3
● Leviticus 19:35-36
● Deuteronomy 11:1
● Luke 16:10
● Luke 19:8

NO Position Statement:

There's never any justified reason to cheat in school. If your abilities or circumstances require lots of studying to get that B on your math test, then get studying. Cheating may sometimes hurt other people, but it will always hurt the cheater the most. Learning to take shortcuts to success is a bad habit to get into. If you cheat in school, then you'll do it in your family, your job, even in your relationship with God. Cheaters only cheat themselves.

NO Discussion Starters:

● No matter what the circumstances are, cheating is never right.

● Cheaters aren't gaining a good grade, they're losing an education.

● Christians are to be honest always, and so they, especially, should never cheat.

● People who learn to cheat now in small ways will become cheaters in big ways later in life.

● Cheating is a sin.

Bible Passages:

● Malachi 1:12-14
● Genesis 27:1-41
● 1 Samuel 12:3
● Leviticus 19:35-36
● Deuteronomy 11:1
● Luke 16:10
● Luke 19:8

YES Position Statement:

Grades mean nothing after you graduate. But junior and senior high school years only come around once, so people need to get the best experience they can during those years.

When grades become the center of a person's school life, there is no social or recreational life. And both those aspects of the junior high and high school experience are critical to personal development.

If you have to make a choice, it's best to spend just enough time on grades to get through school, and plenty of time experiencing the social, recreational and emotional aspects of school life.

YES Discussion Starters:

- Grades are soon forgotten, but memories last.
- Your high school grades won't help you get a better job.
- There's nothing worse than getting straight A's and having no friends.
- People who spend all their time studying miss out on life.
- As long as you're learning, what difference do grades make?

Bible Passages:

- Philippians 4:8
- Titus 3:8
- Titus 2:7
- 1 Timothy 4:12
- 2 Corinthians 13:11
- Proverbs 9:9
- Proverbs 1:5
- Proverbs 8:10

IS THE EXPERIENCE OF GOING TO SCHOOL MORE IMPORTANT THAN GETTING GOOD GRADES?

No

NO Position Statement:

There's no law that says you can't work at getting good grades and enjoy the experiences of school, too. But the best direction for the pendulum to swing is toward the good grades. A solid grade point average will improve a person's chances of getting into a good college or getting a good job. And the skills people learn through studying will go with them long after the grades are forgotten.

Good grades can open doors that stay locked for people who graduate with nothing but an abundance of school memories.

NO Discussion Starters:

● Good grades can get you into good colleges.

● Employers look at grades to see how hard you might work at their companies.

● The skills learned through studying are invaluable and useful in the "real world."

● People can work at getting good grades without completely sacrificing a social life.

Bible Passages:

● Philippians 4:8
● Titus 3:8
● Titus 2:7
● 1 Timothy 4:12
● 2 Corinthians 13:11
● Proverbs 9:9
● Proverbs 1:5
● Proverbs 8:10

IS IT BEST TO TAKE A YEAR OFF FROM SCHOOL BEFORE GOING TO COLLEGE?

Yes

YES Position Statement:

The senior year in high school is a roller-coaster ride of tests, dances, dates and football games. And the prospect of hurling headlong into an even more tumultuous time in three months should make high school graduates stop and think.

A year off from school between high school and college allows people breathing time—and thinking time. And the year off can also help the person save up enough money to go to college in the first place.

YES Discussion Starters:

- A year off gives breathing space.
- Most college freshmen don't know what they want to do for a career until later anyway.
- A year off is another year of savings to go toward college.
- If you go right into college after high school, you don't have time to explore your interests.
- A year of work gives you practical experience that's important in getting a job later.

Bible Passages:

- Philippians 2:3-4
- Titus 3:8
- 1 Timothy 4:12
- 2 Corinthians 13:11
- Proverbs 9:9
- Ephesians 6:1-3
- Proverbs 8:10
- Colossians 4:5

NO Position Statement:

If you take one year off from school after high school graduation, you may be tempted to take off a second year. And a third. Before you know it, the dream of being a lawyer is replaced out of necessity with the reality of being the lawyer's gardener.

Moving from high school into college is a difficult transition, but most freshmen discover quickly what it'll take to succeed—both in college and in life. Momentum is the key to being successful in school. Besides, if you skip a year, then you'll be older than all the other freshmen when you do decide to go.

NO Discussion Starters:

● If you get out of the habit of going to school, it's tough to get back into it.

● Most schools offer on-the-job experiences to improve your chances of getting a job after graduation.

● If you skip a year, your peers will always be ahead of you in school.

● The Bible encourages Christians to seek wisdom at all cost.

Bible Passages:

● Philippians 2:3-4
● Titus 3:8
● 1 Timothy 4:12
● 2 Corinthians 13:11
● Proverbs 9:9
● Ephesians 6:1-3
● Proverbs 8:10
● Colossians 4:5

YES Position Statement:

There's nothing wrong with making more money because more money gives you more opportunities in life.

And the more opportunities you have, the better chance you have of discovering what you really like to do. Plus, a good paying job can help people feel comfortable in life and allow them to share more with people in need. For this reason, making more money is the best motivation for furthering your education.

Money can't buy happiness, but it can afford more chances to find happiness.

YES Discussion Starters:

- The more money someone makes, the more he or she can give to charity and the church.
- Making a good living isn't a sin.
- People need to be honest about the role money plays in their decisions.
- Money, not the joy of learning, pays the bills.
- It's fine to pursue making money—as long as it's not replacing God in your life.

Bible Passages:

- Psalm 62:10
- Job 31:16-25
- Zephaniah 1:18
- 1 Chronicles 29:3-5
- 1 Chronicles 29:12
- Proverbs 15:14
- Proverbs 24:4
- Proverbs 19:8
- Luke 16:1-13
- Mark 10:17-30

IS THE PROSPECT OF MAKING MORE MONEY THE BEST REASON TO FURTHER YOUR EDUCATION?

No

NO Position Statement:

When people choose to further their education, they choose to explore new areas of knowledge. The main goal of education is to facilitate that exploration. But if you focus on the goal of making more money, you may miss the joy of learning along the way.

Getting a good salary is often a result of higher education, but understanding what was taught in school is what will get that job in the first place.

Knowledge should be the main motivator in furthering your education. People who are just out to make money have their priorities out of order.

NO Discussion Starters:

● Learning is the goal of education.
● People who focus on making more money often miss the joy of learning.
● Helping people should be a significant goal of education.
● Learning about life is a better goal than making lots of money.
● If greed motivates you to get an education, then it will probably motivate everything else in your life later on.

Bible Passages:

● Psalm 62:10
● Job 31:16-25
● Zephaniah 1:18
● 1 Chronicles 29:3-5
● 1 Chronicles 29:12

● Proverbs 15:14
● Proverbs 24:4
● Proverbs 19:8
● Luke 16:1-13
● Mark 10:17-30

Scientific and Medical Issues

● Is it ethical to test drugs on animals to identify potential health risks for people?

● Is it ethical for science to manipulate human genes to create "better" people?

● Should the FDA allow a "suicide" pill to be made available to the general public?

● Is euthanasia ethical?

YES Position Statement:

Let's stop all this "save the animals" stuff right now. People, not laboratory rats, were created in God's image.

Researchers can't know for sure about the effects of a drug without first testing that product on a living creature. And since testing the product on people might have adverse effects, such as killing them, the only alternative is to test the drug on animals.

It's okay to risk the health of an animal for the safety of humans.

YES Discussion Starters:

- Laboratories often breed their own animals for testing.
- Safety for people is more important than safety for animals.
- People need medical research to help them overcome serious illnesses.
- God gave people rule over all the animals.
- Animals don't have souls.

Bible Passages:

- Genesis 1:24-26
- Deuteronomy 14:3-21
- Genesis 6:19-21
- Psalm 104:24-32
- Psalm 90:1-17
- Ecclesiastes 3:3

IS IT ETHICAL TO TEST DRUGS ON ANIMALS TO IDENTIFY POTENTIAL HEALTH RISKS FOR PEOPLE?

NO Position Statement:

Who gave humans the right to use animals as living petri dishes? God put animals on the earth first, then gave charge of caring for them to humans. No matter how you look at it, risking animals' lives doesn't sound much like caring for them.

Death is a natural part of life—for both animals and humans. It's fine to try to find cures for the diseases that affect people, but it's not right to cruelly inject animals with those same diseases just to see if they'll live or die.

We must find ways to cure the diseases that afflict us. But we must not kill other living creatures in the process. It's not right.

NO Discussion Starters:

● God commands us to care for the animals.
● Creative testing methods should be devised that don't hurt animals.
● We can't justify killing animals just to make our lives better.
● God created animals. They have a right to live, too.

Bible Passages:

● Genesis 1:24-26
● Deuteronomy 14:3-21
● Genesis 6:19-21
● Psalm 104:24-32
● Psalm 90:1-17
● Ecclesiastes 3:3

Yes

YES Position Statement:

Creative manipulation of human genes is just another example of the creativity God instilled in humankind. God created an intelligent people, and that intelligence is leading us to new biotechnologies.

God created us in his image, and that includes the ability to improve ourselves. There's nothing antibiblical about exploring ways to improve people. In some ways, it's a step in the right direction. If we can eliminate all health problems (physical and mental) before someone is born, the world will become a happier and more productive place.

Isn't that the kind of world God would want us to work toward?

YES Discussion Starters:

● Gene manipulation will eliminate many inherited diseases or conditions.

● Gene manipulation can create healthy people.

● Improving the physical health of people will improve their mental health.

● God is a creative God and probably smiles down on science's latest discoveries.

● By working to eliminate disease and other common human frailties, we're actually working toward the kind of world God wants for us.

Bible Passages:

● Genesis 1:26-31
● Exodus 15:26
● Psalm 8:1-9
● Ecclesiastes 12:1
● Romans 1:25
● 1 Corinthians 6:19-20
● Philippians 1:20
● 1 Corinthians 1:27-31
● James 1:14-15

IS IT ETHICAL FOR SCIENCE TO MANIPULATE HUMAN GENES TO CREATE "BETTER" PEOPLE?

NO Position Statement:

No

When scientists mess with the way people are created, they're playing with God's creation. And that's not right.

If the goal of gene manipulation is to create healthier people, there are other methods to reach that goal: education, health maintenance programs and a pollution-free environment. But if the goal is to create "superpeople," then there's an ethical problem.

God created people in his image. Shouldn't that be good enough?

NO Discussion Starters:

● God created people and liked what he created.
● People can feel good about themselves without the aid of science.
● Messing around with people is like playing God.
● Humans don't have the right to challenge what God has already created.
● People may misuse the process of gene manipulation for their own selfish reasons.

Bible Passages:

● Genesis 1:26-31
● Exodus 15:26
● Psalm 8:1-9
● Ecclesiastes 12:1
● Romans 1:25

● 1 Corinthians 6:19-20
● Philippians 1:20
● 1 Corinthians 1:27-31
● James 1:14-15

YES Position Statement:

If a suicide pill were made available through psychiatrists (by prescription only), people who were considering taking their own lives would be inclined to go to a counselor for the "easy way out." This would create an opportunity for the psychiatrist to counsel the person and potentially turn his or her life around. There is no such checkpoint available today.

In addition, people who are terminally ill could consult a psychiatrist and then make their own choice about how they will live or die. To take away that choice is to burden them with a life of pain.

YES Discussion Starters:

● Some suicides might be stopped if doctors had a chance to talk to the suicidal person.

● Terminally ill people could choose to stop their pain immediately through the use of a suicide pill.

● People should have their own choice about whether to live or die.

● Life is precious, but death is a long and painful process to many people.

Bible Passages:

● Psalm 9:12
● Psalm 42:5
● Lamentations 3:21-27
● Proverbs 19:18

● Matthew 27:3-10
● Romans 8:18-39
● 1 Corinthians 15:54-57

70

NO Position Statement:

Suicide is one of the leading causes of death among young people. To approve of the concept of suicide on any level is to say "killing yourself is a viable option" to today's kids. Even the most depressed person can discover hope again because God can overcome any problem. And Christians can be the catalyst to spreading that good news to all the hopeless people.

Besides, if you created such a pill, who could you trust to administer it fairly? Doctors? The church? No one should be asked to willingly participate in another person's suicidal behavior.

NO Discussion Starters:

- Life is precious.
- Only God has the right to decide when a person dies.
- Suicide is a selfish act.
- There's always hope in every situation.
- Doctors shouldn't have the decision-making power on life and death.

Bible Passages:

- Psalm 9:12
- Psalm 42:5
- Lamentations 3:21-27
- Proverbs 19:18
- Matthew 27:3-10
- Romans 8:18-39
- 1 Corinthians 15:54-57

YES Position Statement:

Yes

Perhaps the better question here is, "Is prolonging life by heroic means ethical?" What benefit do people gain when they're forced to stay alive by artificial means? The cost soon becomes burdensome to the people paying the bills, and the chance for complete recovery often diminishes with each day. It's sad that humankind is anything but "kind" to humanity when it comes to prolonging life. We're more humane to our animals than we are to other people.

It's time to pull the plug on the idea that euthanasia is wrong.

YES Discussion Starters:

- The cost of keeping someone alive is astronomical.
- Quality of life is as important as quantity of life.
- After serious consideration, relatives should have the option of removing life support systems.
- People in comas or people who are constantly sedated because of extreme pain may not want to live, anyway.
- It's humane to remove suffering from people.

Bible Passages:

- Psalm 9:12
- Luke 8:50-56
- 2 Timothy 2:10
- Proverbs 19:18
- Acts 8:7-8
- Romans 8:18-39
- 2 Thessalonians 1:4

NO Position Statement:

There's always a chance—even if it's a small chance—that a person will recover from a terminal illness or a coma. To decide for a person that his or her life isn't worth fighting for takes away that slim chance.

Doctors are sworn to protect and uphold life. Their duty is to find ways to keep people alive. And there are many stories of how God used medicine to bring a terminally ill person (or a person in a coma) back to life.

God has performed lesser miracles throughout history. To kill someone under the guise of euthanasia is to play God and say, "There will be no healing today."

NO Discussion Starters:

- God can heal all illnesses.
- People shouldn't be able to choose whether someone else will live or die.
- Medicine is always improving and may find cures for otherwise terminal diseases.
- It's a doctor's duty to preserve life.
- Miracles do happen.

Bible Passages:

- Psalm 9:12
- Luke 8:50-56
- 2 Timothy 2:10
- Proverbs 19:18
- Acts 8:7-8
- Romans 8:18-39
- 2 Thessalonians 1:4

Sexuality Issues

- Is sex before marriage wrong?

- Should schools be allowed to distribute condoms?

- Should homosexual couples be allowed to marry and raise children?

- Is abortion always wrong?

YES Position Statement:

Saving sex for marriage is a concept that goes back to the book of Genesis. But that doesn't make it an outdated concept.

There's no other way to look at it: Having sex outside of marriage compromises the marriage bed and God's commands.

Wouldn't it be fantastic if everyone waited until marriage before having sex? Spouses would be more fulfilled. Movies, television and music would have to change their content to reflect the positive moral status of our world. Sexually transmitted diseases, such as AIDS, would all but halt their spread.

And couples would be truly happy.

YES Discussion Starters:

● Sex is a powerful thing.

● The only reason to have sex outside of marriage is selfishness.

● It doesn't make sense to commit to someone physically if you're not ready to commit to them in marriage.

● Relationships should be built on communication and love—not sex.

● Sexually transmitted diseases would diminish if people stopped having sex outside of marriage.

● Sex is something so special that it should only be shared with a lifetime partner.

Bible Passages:

● 2 Samuel 11:1-5, 27
● Psalm 51:1-19
● Song of Solomon 5:2-6
● Genesis 2:23-25
● Proverbs 6:20-25

● Matthew 5:27-30
● 1 Corinthians 10:11-13
● 1 Corinthians 13:1-13
● Hebrews 12:12-13

NO Position Statement:

No

Waiting until a paper is signed and for a minister to say, "I now pronounce you husband and wife" is no different from waiting until the "right moment" for sex. For some people, that right moment happens on their wedding night. For others, it can happen long before then.

As long as two people love each other, sex can be a positive part of their relationship. The Bible's warnings about sex are outdated and inappropriate in today's society.

That's not to say that sex is okay any time. People who want to have sex must truly love each other. And they must be in full agreement about having sex.

NO Discussion Starters:

- Sex is okay if two people love each other.
- Sex is okay if people use proper birth control.
- God created sexuality to be explored.
- Why does a marriage license make having sex any more moral?
- Responsible sex can't hurt anyone.
- Couples need to experiment with sexuality before getting married.

Bible Passages:

- 2 Samuel 11:1-5, 27
- Psalm 51:1-19
- Song of Solomon 5:2-6
- Genesis 2:23-25
- Proverbs 6:20-25
- Matthew 5:27-30
- 1 Corinthians 10:11-13
- 1 Corinthians 13:1-13
- Hebrews 12:12-13

YES Position Statement:

With the ongoing concern over AIDS and other sexually transmitted diseases, it only makes sense to help sexually active kids by teaching them about safe sex.

It's unrealistic to expect teenagers to abstain from sexual activity. We can assume most teenagers will probably have sex at least once during their high school years.

Making condoms available to teenagers doesn't promote sexual activity; it simply reminds kids of the seriousness of sex and helps them avoid the dangers of unprotected sex.

Condoms can save lives. So what's wrong with making them available at school?

YES Discussion Starters:

● The use of condoms significantly reduces the chance for getting sexually transmitted diseases.

● Kids could get condoms somewhere else anyway.

● Schools can provide condoms along with education about safe sex.

● Most teenagers are sexually active by the time they finish high school.

● Condoms remind kids to be responsible about sex.

Bible Passages:

● Proverbs 16:17
● Ecclesiastes 2:1-11
● Proverbs 2:11
● 2 Samuel 11:1-5, 27
● Song of Solomon 5:2-6
● Genesis 2:23-25
● Proverbs 6:20-25
● Matthew 5:27-30
● 1 Corinthians 10:11-13
● 1 Corinthians 13:1-13

NO Position Statement:

No

The only truly safe sex is no sex.

If the goal in making condoms available at school is to encourage sexual activity, let the schools provide them. But if the goal is to teach responsible sexuality, forget it. Condoms don't teach a thing.

Instead of providing condoms to kids at school, let's see the schools take a stronger stance and encourage abstinence. People once laughed at the concept of "waiting until marriage." But with AIDS on the rise, it's time to do what's best for kids rather than just encouraging their dangerous behavior. Teach abstinence; don't distribute condoms in schools.

NO Discussion Starters:

● The Bible condemns sexual activity outside of marriage.

● Condoms may limit sexually transmitted diseases, but they do nothing to eliminate the emotional trauma of having sex before marriage.

● Safe sex with condoms is a myth.

● Parents, not schools, should shape kids' sexual attitudes.

● Kids aren't responsible enough to use condoms every time they have sex, anyway.

Bible Passages:

● Proverbs 16:17
● Ecclesiastes 2:1-11
● Proverbs 2:11
● 2 Samuel 11:1-5, 27
● Song of Solomon 5:2-6

● Genesis 2:23-25
● Proverbs 6:20-25
● Matthew 5:27-30
● 1 Corinthians 10:11-13
● 1 Corinthians 13:1-13

YES Position Statement:

Homosexuality is becoming an accepted lifestyle in our society. And even though many Christians challenge the appropriateness of homosexuality, they can't deny that homosexual people have rights, too.

If homosexual couples want to marry and raise children, that's their right. Who's to judge how "good" or "bad" a homosexual couple might be as parents? Since homosexual couples must decide to be parents, they probably know what they're getting into. That can't be said of all heterosexual couples.

This issue isn't about whether homosexuality is wrong. It's about equal rights for everyone—even people we disagree with.

YES Discussion Starters:

● Homosexuals have rights, too.

● Children need good parents, but that doesn't mean the parents have to be heterosexual.

● Marriage is a personal thing, so Christians ought to let people marry whoever they want.

● The government shouldn't be allowed to legislate who can and can't get married.

Bible Passages:

● Genesis 1:27-28
● Genesis 19:1-38
● Leviticus 18:22
● Romans 1:26-27

● Psalm 108:4
● 1 Corinthians 13:1-13
● Colossians 3:11

SHOULD HOMOSEXUAL COUPLES BE ALLOWED TO MARRY AND RAISE CHILDREN?

NO Position Statement:

"This is my mom...and this is my other mom."

The warped sense of family brought upon by two dads or two moms will undoubtedly affect the children. Who will teach the children about the role of the dad if there is no dad? How will the child discover the importance of motherhood if there is no mother?

Children need to grow up with the idea that a family includes mom, dad and the kids. Homosexual couples can't provide that.

NO Discussion Starters:

● Homosexual couples can't provide a balanced perspective on what family is all about.

● The Bible calls homosexuality a sin.

● Children raised in a homosexual environment would have a difficult time discovering their true identity as a male or female.

Bible Passages:

● Genesis 1:27-28
● Genesis 19:1-38
● Leviticus 18:22
● Romans 1:26-27

● Psalm 108:4
● 1 Corinthians 13:1-13
● Colossians 3:11

81

YES Position Statement:

No human being has the right to take the life of another. And that includes abortion.

Without exception, the life of the baby is what's most important in the issue of abortion. Of course, if both the mother's and the baby's lives are in jeopardy, the mother's life must be saved first. But to simply allow people to "cancel" their mistakes or change their minds about bearing children is advocating murder.

The growing child has no say in the matter of abortion. And so, taking that child's life is akin to shooting someone in the back. There is no middle ground on this issue: Abortion is murder.

YES Discussion Starters:

- Abortion is murder.
- Murder goes against the teaching of the Bible.
- Allowing people the option to kill unborn children takes away the need for responsible sexual behavior.
- If the mother truly doesn't want the child, she can always give him or her up for adoption.

Bible Passages:

- Exodus 20:13
- Zechariah 7:8-10
- Psalm 139:13-16
- Matthew 25:31-40
- Proverbs 16:1-3
- Genesis 1:28
- Deuteronomy 30:19-20
- Jeremiah 1:5

NO Position Statement:

Women should have the choice to do what they want with their bodies. To make abortion illegal is to strip women of that right.

One thing that separates humans from the animal world is the ability to choose freely. And whether or not you personally believe in abortion, by making it illegal you steal the element of free choice from those individuals. And you force them into committing "illegal" acts.

Abortion should be a matter of personal choice...not a matter for the courts to decide.

NO Discussion Starters:

● Women will have abortions even if it becomes illegal, but the health hazards will increase.

● Women should be able to do what they want with their bodies.

● Abortion isn't murder.

● Aborted fetuses aren't really babies yet, anyway.

● Abortion can save a potential mother from the trauma of caring for a child she doesn't want.

● Abortion may be the best option in rape cases.

Bible Passages:

● Exodus 20:13
● Zechariah 7:8-10
● Psalm 139:13-16
● Matthew 25:31-40
● Proverbs 16:1-3
● Genesis 1:28
● Deuteronomy 30:19-20
● Jeremiah 1:5

Social and Political Issues

● Does the government perpetuate the problem of poverty by providing money for the poor?

● Is war always wrong?

● Would stricter gun control laws reduce the number of violent crimes?

● Should the government spend millions of dollars on military defense?

● Do the courts have the right to choose death as punishment for a serious crime?

DOES THE GOVERNMENT PERPETUATE THE PROBLEM OF POVERTY BY PROVIDING MONEY FOR THE POOR?

YES Position Statement:

Yes

By continuing to support the poor through welfare and other programs, the government ensures that poor people will always be with us. Instead of providing monetary support, the government should provide programs to help educate the poor. Money and other material charity simply serve to encourage people not to find work or further their education.

We need to stop encouraging poor people to remain poor. Instead, we must educate and prepare poor people to make a valuable contribution to our society.

YES Discussion Starters:

- Charity encourages people to seek handouts instead of work.
- Appropriate education can help poor people find work.
- Self-esteem comes from making a contribution to society—not from taking charity.
- If there were no option for people to get money except through working, more people would find a job.
- Many poor people are poor because they've learned to depend on the government.

Bible Passages:

- Deuteronomy 15:11
- Exodus 23:11
- Psalm 9:18
- Proverbs 6:6-11
- Matthew 25:31-46
- Mark 6:30-44
- 2 Corinthians 8:8-9
- Mark 14:7
- James 2:14-17

NO Position Statement:

By eliminating benefits for poor people, the government only serves to create poorer people. Most poor people are poor because of lost jobs, inadequate schooling or long-gone spouses. And without the benefits provided by government programs, these people would die of starvation.

Jesus said, "You will always have poor people." But Jesus also commanded his people to care for the poor.

NO Discussion Starters:

● Christians should help the poor as much as possible.

● Poor people would have no opportunity for income without government assistance.

● Poverty isn't usually the result of laziness.

● Poverty won't be solved by cutting off assistance but by adding educational incentives to the monetary support.

Bible Passages:

● Deuteronomy 15:11
● Exodus 23:11
● Psalm 9:18
● Proverbs 6:6-11
● Matthew 25:31-46

● Mark 6:30-44
● 2 Corinthians 8:8-9
● Mark 14:7
● James 2:14-17

YES Position Statement:

No reason for war is ever good enough to compensate for the loss of hundreds and even thousands of lives. Each dead soldier leaves family behind who will never see him or her again. That's a terrible price to pay for the rights to an oil-producing country or for an additional 10 miles of border property. There are always alternatives to war. Trade embargoes can quickly squeeze a country into a retreating position. And well-crafted treaties can often solve problems before they turn into battles.

War never solves problems—it just shows who has the most soldiers to spare.

YES Discussion Starters:

- Death is the only sure thing about a war.
- Countries should seek peaceful solutions to all disagreements.
- If less money were spent on weapons, countries would have fewer methods to fight wars.
- War is simply a political weapon.
- No one ever wins a war.

Bible Passages:

- Joshua 6:1-27
- 1 Samuel 17:1-50
- Jeremiah 7:5-7
- Psalm 34:14
- Joel 3:9-17

- 1 Timothy 2:2
- Ecclesiastes 3:8
- Isaiah 2:4
- Hebrews 12:14

NO Position Statement:

No

While it's always a last resort, war isn't always wrong. Sometimes the only way to get someone's attention is to drop a bomb on him or her.

When one nation is testing its power at the expense of a weaker nation, someone has to step in and remind the power-hungry nation to back off. Embargoes and friendly discussions might help, but a show of force is often the only alternative that gets the power-hungry nation's attention.

War is sometimes the only way to stop evil people from spreading their influence.

NO Discussion Starters:

- War can put an end to corrupt governments.
- Soldiers don't die in vain; they die protecting freedom.
- War is a quick solution to political unrest.
- Peace can sometimes only come from a show of military strength.
- There are some things worth fighting for.

Bible Passages:

- Joshua 6:1-27
- 1 Samuel 17:1-50
- Jeremiah 7:5-7
- Psalm 34:14
- Joel 3:9-17

- 1 Timothy 2:2
- Ecclesiastes 3:8
- Isaiah 2:4
- Hebrews 12:14

YES Position Statement:

Imagine this scene: After an explosive argument, a distraught husband walks into a gun shop and purchases a revolver and ammunition. With little thought, he marches back to his home and opens fire on his wife and family, then turns the gun on himself. In a matter of minutes, a family is destroyed by a hail of bullets.

This extreme case illustrates just one good reason for strict gun control laws. With tighter reigns on purchasing guns, many violent crimes (especially domestic crimes) could be avoided. It's just like reducing the speed limit: Even if one life is saved, it's worth the inconvenience to everyone else.

YES Discussion Starters:

● People don't have to think twice about using a gun if it's readily available.

● Without easy access to guns, people might actually talk through their problems.

● TV shows have wrongly convinced people that shooting people is a normal occurrence.

● The only reason people challenge gun control is because of their own impatience and inconvenience.

● Violence of any kind is never the answer to problems.

Bible Passages:

● Matthew 26:51-54
● Joel 3:9-17
● Ecclesiastes 9:18
● 2 Corinthians 10:1-6
● John 10:10
● Micah 4:3
● Ezekiel 43:9

WOULD STRICTER GUN CONTROL LAWS REDUCE THE NUMBER OF VIOLENT CRIMES?

NO Position Statement:

Even if we could magically take all the guns in the world away, there would always be violent crimes. Instead of guns, people would grab knives, clubs or even the nearest trash can to inflict pain on their victims.

Guns aren't the cause of violent crimes—people are. So the only way to reduce violent crimes is to educate or get rid of people. Besides, criminals who want guns can always find them through the black market or other illegal sources.

NO Discussion Starters:

- Guns don't kill—people do.
- Most gun purchasers are responsible people.
- Why should the majority of gun enthusiasts suffer because of a few "bad eggs"?
- Gun control won't keep criminals from getting guns.
- Enacting stricter gun control laws is like treating the symptom, not the cause, of violent crimes.

Bible Passages:

- Matthew 26:51-54
- Joel 3:9-17
- Ecclesiastes 9:18
- 2 Corinthians 10:1-6
- John 10:10
- Micah 4:3
- Ezekiel 43:9

YES Position Statement:

Yes

A strong defense is the best offense.

If other countries had no multiple war-head missiles, aircraft carriers or close-strike gunships, defense spending could probably be cut to nearly nothing.

But there are weapons. All over the world. And the moment we decide to let the tanks rust, other countries who may be less "polite" about their weapons may decide to overrun our country. Our freedom is worth the cost of the defense budget.

YES Discussion Starters:

● Whether we like it or not, weapons of war are a reality in our world, and they're not going to go away.

● Defense spending ensures peace.

● We must match or exceed other countries' military technology.

● A strong military defense encourages other countries to find peaceful solutions to their problems.

Bible Passages:

● Psalm 37:37
● Psalm 147:14
● 2 Chronicles 32:7-8
● Isaiah 59:18
● Luke 10:19
● 1 Timothy 2:2
● James 3:18
● 1 Kings 4:20-28

No

NO Position Statement:

Peace isn't going to happen until countries "turn their swords into plowshares." And someone has to go first.

It's no secret that there's enough firepower in the world to destroy the whole planet many times over. So why do we continue to spend money on military defense? If our government began spending that money elsewhere (on research for cures to diseases or on education), perhaps other world powers would catch on.

A huge military budget may help to maintain "forced" peace, but trust brings real peace. Why don't we take the first step toward building that trust?

NO Discussion Starters:

- The more weapons we have, the more chances they'll be used.
- Peace can't really be forced upon people.
- Reduced defense spending makes more money available for education and other more important needs.
- A strong defense program just shows a lack of understanding of what real peace is all about.

Bible Passages:

- Psalm 37:37
- Psalm 147:14
- 2 Chronicles 32:7-8
- Isaiah 59:18
- Luke 10:19
- 1 Timothy 2:2
- James 3:18
- 1 Kings 4:20-28

DO THE COURTS HAVE THE RIGHT TO CHOOSE DEATH AS PUNISHMENT FOR A SERIOUS CRIME?

YES Position Statement:

The Old Testament clearly identifies death as an appropriate punishment for a murderer. And in society today, where murder is an all-too-common occurrence, there's no reason to ignore that teaching. Rather than sentencing murderers to something as ridiculous as 12 consecutive life sentences, we should strip them of the right they took from someone else—the right to life.

The death penalty may also serve as a deterrent to criminals. By telling would-be murderers up front that they'll be put to death if they kill someone, they may think twice before pulling the trigger.

YES Discussion Starters:

● Our prisons are overcrowded as it is.
● Death is a fair price to pay for robbing someone else of life.
● The Bible illustrates many reasons for taking the life of a murderer.
● Rehabilitation is rarely possible with violent criminals.
● Justice requires that we take serious action in serious circumstances.

Bible Passages:

● Leviticus 24:21
● Exodus 21:12
● Numbers 35:16-25
● Deuteronomy 30:20
● Ezekiel 18:23
● Micah 6:8
● Micah 7:18
● Matthew 12:7
● James 2:13

NO Position Statement:

No one has the right to take another person's life. That's the reason murderers are put in jail in the first place. If we decide our courts can have the right to take another person's life, we're advocating the same kind of wrong behavior we're punishing murderers for.

There is no justification for killing another person, no matter how harsh the crime. Rehabilitation is a possibility we can't rob from murderers. God alone has the wisdom to impart justice that would require the death of the accused.

NO Discussion Starters:

- We can't play God and decide who lives and dies.
- There is always a possibility the accused murderer is innocent.
- The death penalty may be biblical, but so is mercy.
- Love should be able to overcome all wrongs.
- The death penalty gives the courts too much power.

Bible Passages:

- Leviticus 24:21
- Exodus 21:12
- Numbers 35:16-25
- Deuteronomy 30:20
- Ezekiel 18:23
- Micah 6:8
- Micah 7:18
- Matthew 12:7
- James 2:13

Part Two:

**Bonus Discussion-
Starter Activities**

Faith Issues

Looking for Answers

Get permission to take your kids to a Buddhist temple or another non-Christian place of worship. Encourage kids to take notes and ask questions to find out what the worshipers truly believe. Then meet back at church and discuss the following questions:

- **What did you learn about this religion?**
- **What role does worship play in these people's lives?**
- **What are the similarities between this religion and Christianity? What are the differences?**
- **How did you feel in this new environment?**
- **Does it seem these people are worshiping the same God as Christians? Why or why not?**

Faith Talk

Invite a member of a non-Christian religion to speak and answer questions at a youth group meeting. Have kids come up with their own questions to ask. Include questions such as:

- **Why do you believe what you do?**
- **What is the history of your religion?**
- **What makes your religion unique?**
- **How does your religion view Christianity?**

Create-a-Cult

Form groups of no more than four and give each group a Bible and a concordance. Say: **Your job is to create a cult by searching out odd passages and pulling them out of context to create your doctrine. You can use any passages you want to define your group. Also, come up with a name for your cult and a list of three or four things you teach.**

After groups have created their cults, have them present the information to the whole group. Then ask:

- **What did you discover about cults in this activity?**
- **How did you feel as you created your cult?**
- **How is the way you created a cult like the way cults might actually develop?**
- **What dangers are there in taking scriptures out of context?**

Church Attendance

Form a number of small groups (no more than six kids per group) and have a few people sit by themselves outside of the groups. Give groups and individuals each a Bible. Say: **Your assignment is to discuss Matthew 5:1-12 and decide what it means for people today. If you're in a small group, you may discuss this issue and come to an agreement on what you believe. But if you're not in a group, you must come to a conclusion on your own.**

After about 10 minutes, call time and have groups and individuals share their conclusions. Then ask the groups:

● **How did you feel working together on this assignment?**

● **How did you help each other find insights into this passage?**

Ask the individuals:

● **How did you feel working on your own?**

Ask everyone:

● **How is the way the small groups worked like the way a church is supposed to work?**

● **What benefits did the small group have that the individual didn't?**

● **What does this activity say about the importance of church attendance?**

Border Patrol

Create a simulation for kids to experience the dangers and threats of illegally smuggling Bibles across a border. Go to a nearby park or open field and set up sentries (adult sponsors who will act as the border patrol) and a beginning and ending place for the smugglers. Add whatever elements you want to make the situation realistic, but let kids know what you're doing ahead of time so no one is alarmed.

Afterward, ask:

● **How did you feel as you tried to smuggle the Bibles?**

● **Is it okay for Christians to smuggle Bibles even though it's against the local country's laws?**

● **What legal ways could you have used to get the Bibles to Christians in the other country?**

Health Issues

Body Beautiful?

Form groups of no more than five and have groups each pick their contestant for a Body Beautiful competition. Provide cloth, paper, markers and other items. Encourage groups to turn their contestants into "perfect bodies" using the provided materials. You might want to have only guys be contestants to avoid embarrassing depictions of the perfect female body.

Then have groups each present their contestant. Have votes on the winner of the contest and award that person a box of cookies.

Have kids return to their groups to discuss the following questions:

● **How did you feel during this contest?**

● **How is this contest like the way people try to look good in real life?**

● **How are the shortcuts you took in creating your contestant like the shortcuts people take in real life?**

● **The winner was rewarded with a box of cookies. What rewards do people look for in real life when they try to improve their looks?**

Can't Eat Just One

Form groups of no more than five and give each group a bowl of potato chips. Say: **Pass the chips around your group and let each person take just one chip and eat it. Then pass the chips around again and take one each, but just hold it. You may not eat the second chip.**

Ask:

● **How easy is it to stop after eating just one chip?**

● **How do you feel holding a second chip knowing that you can't eat it?**

● **How are these feelings like the way people who take drugs might feel?**

● **What is the attraction of eating potato chips?**

● **How is that like the attraction of taking drugs?**

Drink?

Have kids role play the following situations and discuss how realistic each one is. Then have kids discuss the questions listed at the end of each role-play situation.

Situation One: You're at a party with a bunch of your friends. None of you is old enough to drink alcohol legally, but most of the people are drinking. What do you do when a friend comes up and offers you a beer?

Discussion questions:
- **Is it okay to break the law when it comes to drinking?**
- **Why do teenagers drink?**
- **What's the best way to say no to drinking?**

Situation Two: You're 22 years old, out of college and have just begun working for a small accounting firm. It's Friday evening and you're planning a couch-potato TV marathon at your apartment. Your roommate left you a bottle of wine and some cheese and crackers to help you celebrate your lack of a date. Do you pop open the bottle of wine?

Discussion questions:
- **Is it okay to drink alone?**
- **Is it okay to drink alcohol but hide it from your fellow Christians?**

Situation Three: You're married and working for a large insurance corporation. You've been invited to a social event by your boss. When you arrive, everyone in the room is holding some kind of drink or another. Do you step over to the bar to get one for yourself, too?

Discussion questions:
- **When, if ever, is social drinking okay? Explain.**
- **Is it better to stand out because you don't drink, or to fit in by drinking? Explain.**
- **Is having an occasional drink any better or worse than drinking with your friends every weekend? Explain.**

What's Up, Doc?

Have a doctor visit your group to talk about the physical effects of drugs and alcohol. Invite kids to come up with their own questions to ask the doctor. Include questions such as:
- **When is someone considered legally drunk?**
- **What are the long-term side effects of taking drugs?**

Media Issues

Video Review

Get parents' permission to show a number of video clips to kids from movies with different ratings (G, PG, PG-13 and R). Preview scenes from each film and cue up representative scenes for kids to view and discuss.

Before watching the clips, have kids form groups of three or four. Then have groups each watch and assign a rating (G, PG, PG-13 or R) to each of the clips they watch. Afterward, tell kids what the rating really was and have them discuss the following questions:

- **What factors should determine a movie rating?**
- **Are some things appropriate for adults but not teenagers? Why or why not?**
- **Does a rating really mean anything to the viewer? Why or why not?**
- **What's the best reason for watching a movie?**
- **What are good reasons for avoiding a movie?**

Lights, Camera, Action!

Form groups of no more than five. Have groups each come up with a basic script idea for a blockbuster film. Encourage kids to base their ideas on what's been successful at the box office in recent months.

Have groups each plan a short scene to enact from their film. Allow about 15 to 20 minutes for groups to come up with their ideas, gather props and practice their scenes. Then have groups each describe their movie and act out their scene for the whole group.

Ask:

- **What elements were similar among all the movies?**
- **What would each movie likely be rated?**
- **How might your parents react to these movies?**
- **How might Jesus react to each of the films?**

Music Comparison

Have kids bring in their favorite CDs or tapes. Play a song from each and have kids evaluate its musical, lyrical and performance merit. For each song, ask the following questions:

- **What kind of message does the song present?**
- **What feelings does the song create in the listener?**

- What's good about the song?
- What's not so good about the song?

Feelings

Play samples of a variety of styles of music for your group, including classical, jazz, country, heavy metal, dance, pop, reggae and any other diverse styles your kids might recommend.

After each song, ask:

- How did this song make you feel? Why?

After you've played all the samples, form groups of no more than five to discuss the following questions:

- How might the feeling you get when you listen to a song influence your attitude in life?
- What positive effects can songs have?
- What negative effects can songs have?

Laugh . . . or Don't

Get parents' permission to play segments of comedy monologues from both "raunchy" comedians and clean comedians. Have kids listen to (carefully edited) segments of the raunchy comedian's monologue and segments of the clean comedian's monologue. Then ask:

- What's different about the humor in these two samples?
- How did both comedians make you feel?
- Which comedian made you feel best? Explain.
- What does this activity say about the appropriateness of listening to raunchy comedians?

The Limits of Friendship

Have kids each tell one nice thing they might do for a friend (anything from helping the friend with homework to buying the friend a new car). Then form pairs and have partners determine what the limits of a friendship should be. Ask these questions to help pairs think about the boundaries of friendship:

● **Is it okay for someone to lie to keep a friend out of trouble? Why or why not?**

● **Would you ever die for a friend? Why or why not?**

● **What do you do if a friend wants you to join him or her in an illegal activity?**

● **When do friends become too needy?**

Have partners share their insights with the whole group.

Milk and Soft Drink

Form two groups. Give members of one group each a half cup of milk and members of the other group each a half cup of orange or grape soft drink. Say: **During this activity, mill around and talk with other people about your worst dating experience or a friend's. Be careful not to spill your soft drink or milk, and don't drink it until I tell you. When I say, "Pair up," find the nearest person and pair up with him or her.**

After a few minutes, say: **Pair up!** Watch as kids find partners. Ask which pairs ended up with the same drink and which ended up with different drinks. Say: **Mix your drink with your partner's and then pour half back into your cup so each person has some of the mixture. And now . . . enjoy! You may drink your liquid.**

Some kids might not want to taste the milk and soft drink mixture, but encourage them to try it anyway.

Form a circle and have kids take turns answering the following questions:

● **How did it feel to end up with a person who had the same kind of drink?**

● **How is that like the way you feel when you meet someone who believes the same things you do?**

● **How did it feel to end up with a person who had a different drink?**

● **How is the way you felt when you tasted the soft drink and**

103

milk mixture like the way people might feel when they're in a relationship with someone who doesn't have the same beliefs?
- **What does this activity tell us about the risks of dating a non-Christian?**

Dorp!

Have kids create their own "swear word." Then give kids the following situations to act out, using the made-up swear word. Remind kids to use only the fake word and not real ones. Use these settings:
- at a sports game,
- in the hallway at school,
- when you're hammering something and miss the nail and
- when you're angry at someone who's wronged you.

After kids role play these scenarios, ask:
- **How did you feel using the fake swear word?**
- **How is that like or unlike the way you feel when someone uses a swear word in real life? Explain.**
- **Why do people use bad language?**
- **When, if ever, might swearing be okay?**

Parents and the Truth

Invite teenagers and parents to a meeting about the importance of telling the truth. Consider using the "Is it ever best to withhold the truth from parents?" discussion starter on page 50 to get things going. Form mixed groups of kids and parents to discuss these questions:
- **Is lying ever okay?**
- **When is lying most dangerous or harmful?**
- **How does it feel when you discover a parent or teenager has lied?**

Allow a time for both parents and kids to make a commitment to be truthful in the future.

I Lied

Begin a meeting by lying to kids about something that happened to you. Say you were mugged or that you won the lottery. After a minute or two, admit your lie and ask:
- **How do you feel now that you know I lied to you?**
- **How is that like the way parents or peers feel when they discover you've lied to them?**
- **What are the dangers of lying?**

School Issues

Cheating Test

Before your meeting, get a copy of a high school math book and create a test using some of the problems from that book. Also, contact one or two students and tell them about the test you'll be giving. Tell these students that they're to obviously cheat during the test to get all the answers right. Let these kids know that the answer sheet is at the front of the room and that you'll leave the room for a few minutes during the test.

When you meet with your group, give kids the test and ask them to complete it. Leave the room for a few minutes to allow your "cheaters" to sneak up and get the answers. After kids have finished the test, collect the papers and skim them before giving out a small prize to your one or two cheaters for getting all the answers right.

Kids will probably expose the cheaters to you. If they don't, fill everyone in on the setup. Then ask:

- **How did you feel when you saw some of the kids cheating?**
- **Did any of you join in their cheating? Why or why not?**
- **How is that like or unlike situations at school? Explain.**
- **Why is it so tempting to cheat at school?**
- **Is it ever okay to cheat? If so, when?**

Best Grade

Play a team-sports game such as volleyball or basketball and encourage kids to compete as much as possible to win. Tell kids you'll award a prize to the team with the most points.

While kids are in the "heat of the battle," call time and have them form a circle for a short discussion. Ask:

- **How do you feel competing in this game?**
- **How is this like or unlike the way you feel about competing in school? Explain.**
- **Which is more important to you in this game, winning or having fun playing? Explain.**
- **When does the desire to get good grades become a dangerous obsession?**

Take a Year Off

Form two groups and have each take one of the following sentences and complete it with as many ideas as they can think of:

- "It's best to take a year off of school between high school and college because..."
- "It's best not to skip a year of school between high school and college because..."

Then have both groups present and compare their lists. Ask kids to explore the pros and cons of both sides. For more insight on this issue, have college-age adults who've experienced each of these options join your meeting to tell about their experiences.

Go for the Candy

Use this activity to enhance a meeting on the importance of material wealth. Toss a bunch of wrapped candy around the room before your meeting. When kids arrive, say: **The candy that's tossed around the room is for whoever grabs it first. However, no one may touch the candy until I say, "Money is everything" sometime during the meeting.**

Continue your meeting as planned. At some time during the meeting, call out: **Money is everything!** Watch kids react. Some will dive for the candy while others sit and ignore it. After the candy has been collected, ask:

- **How did you feel when I called out, "Money is everything"?**
- **How is the way people reacted to the candy like the way people react to the prospect of making lots of money?**

Give kids who collected lots of candy the opportunity to share it with others.

Job Survey

Form pairs and assign each pair a different career to discuss. For example, one pair might have secretary and another might have truck driver. Have pairs discuss the job qualifications and requirements for their assigned careers. Have kids especially focus on the educational requirements and probable salaries for each career.

Bring everyone together and have pairs present their findings. Then ask:

- **What seems to be the most important qualification for your job?**
- **What trends do you notice about the job qualifications we've discussed?**
- **How closely is education tied to potential monetary gain?**

Testing, Testing

Choose three or four volunteers to be your "laboratory rats" for this activity. Let these kids know upfront that their participation might end up a bit messy. Give each of these participants a rain poncho to wear. Say: **Here at Cosmetic Research Incorporated, we're testing a new substance that could solve the problem of acne for good. The problem is that this substance hasn't been tested on humans and might result in injury or other negative side effects. So we're going to test the substance on our laboratory rats first.**

Bring out two hard-boiled eggs and four raw eggs. Don't tell kids which are which. Say: **One possible side effect of this product is chemical leakage that inevitably leads to death. But since we're still in the early development stage of this product, that's a risk we'll have to take.**

Have volunteers each come up, one at a time, choose an egg and "test" the egg by cracking it on a laboratory rat's head. If the egg is raw, that laboratory rat must leave the room (to wash up) and may not return during the discussion time.

After all the lab rats have had a chance to be tested, form a circle and ask:

● **How did you feel as you watched the experiment?**

● **How is this like or unlike the way animals are used in chemical testing? Explain.**

● **How does it feel to have "lost" one or more of your lab rats?**

● **If the cure for acne were finally discovered because of this experiment, would it have been worth it? Why or why not?**

Building the Perfect Human

Form groups of no more than five. Have groups each brainstorm the components of the perfect human. Encourage kids to consider such categories as physical build, mental abilities, personality traits and emotional strengths. One way kids could describe these traits is by comparing them to known people. For example, a group might list the perfect human as having Einstein's intellect, Kevin Costner's eyes and Mother Teresa's compassion.

When groups are done, have them share their perfect people with the whole group. Then ask:

- **If scientists could produce the person you've just described through gene manipulation, should they? Why or why not?**
- **Would you enjoy the freedom to choose the character traits of your own child? Why or why not?**
- **What are the ethical dilemmas involved in gene manipulation?**
- **How might God view science's fascination with gene manipulation?**
- **Is it wrong to want to improve humankind through science? Why or why not?**

Humane?

Take kids on a tour of a local humane society and have a representative explain the euthanasia procedures to the kids. Then have kids visit a terminal-illness ward at a local hospital.

Afterward, have kids explore their feelings about the issue of euthanasia. Start by discussing the following questions:

- **How did you feel at each of these places?**
- **What similarities and differences are there between terminal patients and animals marked for euthanasia? Explain.**
- **Why does society authorize euthanasia for animals but frown upon it for humans?**
- **What's the best way to help people who are terminally ill?**
- **If life is precious, how can people support euthanasia?**

Terminal Thoughts

Have volunteers interview terminally ill patients to discover their feelings on life and death. Then have kids share their interview findings with the whole group.

What Would You Do?

Have kids each share how they'd like to be treated if they were to fall into a coma with little or no chance of coming out of the coma. Ask kids to consider the following questions:

- **Would you want someone to "pull the plug" if keeping you alive meant draining your family's income?**
- **Would you want someone to "pull the plug" if you knew at least two other people had come out of a similar coma?**

Bruised

During this discussion, be especially sensitive to teenagers who may already be sexually active or who have been sexually abused.

Form a circle. Place a fresh peach in the center of the circle on the floor. Hand another fresh peach to the person on your left and encourage him or her to toss it to someone else. Have kids toss, roll and otherwise play with the peach until it begins to show bruises from all the handling.

Then place the two peaches next to each other. Ask:

● **Which peach would you rather eat? Explain.**

● **What makes eating the peach that was handled seem unappealing?**

● **How is the unbruised peach like a virgin?**

● **How is the bruised peach like someone who was careless with his or her sexuality?**

● **How might people who are sexually active feel like this bruised peach?**

After your discussion draws to a close, bring out a third fresh peach and say: **Even if you've been sexually active, God's forgiveness can take away the bruises and make you whole again, just like this new peach.**

Make yourself available after the meeting to talk to kids who might be struggling with the issue of sex.

What's Really Happening?

Have kids develop a simple survey to check teenagers' attitudes toward sex. Include questions such as "Do you believe sex before marriage is okay?" and "When is it okay for someone to have sex?"

Have kids get permission to distribute copies of the survey at school. Then meet to discuss the results with your youth group. Ask:

● **How do the findings in your survey compare with what you thought kids might say?**

● **What do the survey results say about teenagers' attitudes toward sex?**

● **Are the results of the survey hopeful or depressing? Explain.**

Homosexuality and Careers

Have kids discuss the following questions in groups of no more than four to explore their feelings about homosexuality:

● **Is homosexuality a sin? Why or why not?**

● **Are there any careers that should be denied to homosexuals? Why or why not?**

● **Should homosexuals try to change their lifestyle and become heterosexual? Why or why not?**

● **Should the church endorse homosexuality as a valid lifestyle? Why or why not?**

Save the Chocolate Chips

Add this activity to a meeting on sex to help kids explore what it's like to deal with sexual temptation. Have kids help you bake chocolate chip cookies during the meeting. Place all the ingredients on a table. Say: **The only rule to follow during this activity is that you can't sample any of the chocolate chips or cookie dough while we're making these cookies. Everyone must wait until the cookies are completely done before eating anything.**

Have kids help out mixing the ingredients and baking the cookies. Keep your eyes open to see if anyone snitches dough or chocolate chips.

When the cookies are in the oven, ask:

● **How easy was it to keep from tasting the chocolate chips or cookie dough?**

● **How is the temptation to taste these ingredients before the cookies are done like the temptation to become sexually active before marriage?**

● **What are practical ways to reduce the temptations to become sexually active?**

When the cookies are done, serve them to the group. Say: **Just as these cookies are worth waiting for, so is the experience of sex.**

Get a Job

Have kids role play a poverty-stricken person seeking employment. Set up the scene by describing the person's lack of training and education. Then have volunteers play the parts of various employers. After the role-plays, ask:

● **What's the government's responsibility to poor people?**
● **How much of poverty is due to laziness?**
● **What can be done to help poor people succeed in life?**
● **Does charity help or hurt the chances for poor people to find self-worth in society? Explain.**

Marshmallow Battle

Form three or four teams and give each a bag of marshmallows. Say: **Each team is a different country. All the countries share at least one border and want to expand their borders. Your marshmallows represent your weapons and you are ready for war, if necessary. In the next five minutes, do what you must to get what your country wants. You may decide to use your marshmallows to battle or bargain with another government. Each person who's hit by two or more marshmallows is out of the activity and must sit or lie still on the floor until the time is up.**

After five minutes, call time and have kids help you evaluate the way each team reacted.

If a war was started, ask:
● **What caused the war to begin?**
● **Was it easy to stay out of the war? Why or why not?**
● **What was the end result of the war?**

If a war wasn't started, ask:
● **Why didn't teams start a war?**
● **What peaceful solutions were discovered to this situation?**

Then ask:
● **How are the decisions in this activity like the decisions made in real life?**
● **What can we learn from this activity about wars?**

Welcome, Alien

Form groups of no more than five. Have groups each choose one person to be the alien for their group. Say: **If our space program** just discovered there really was life on another planet and your group was chosen to be the first to speak to an alien, what would you say to him or her? Explain to your alien about each of the following things and what they mean: war, poverty, faith, love, family, movies, nuclear weapons, abortion and drugs. Add other categories if you want.

After about 10 minutes, have the groups' aliens tell what they heard their groups saying about the issues. Then ask:

● **What might an alien think of the way we behave in our world?**

● **How would you tell an alien about what Jesus did for the world?**

● **What could you say to an alien that would help him or her see the good in people?**

Play and Pay

Form teams and play a game of volleyball. After the game, go around and give each player a specific amount of play money. Tell everyone how much each person gets and make up a reason for giving that amount. For example, you might give one person $100 because he missed a shot and another person $5,000 because she made a great play. It's best not to actually match the dollars to the player's ability so you don't hurt anyone's feelings.

Afterward, ask:

● **How did you feel when you got your money?**

● **How did you feel when you discovered someone else had more money than you?**

● **How is the way money was distributed in this activity like the way professional athletes are paid?**

● **What's good about this system? What's bad?**

● **What would be the wisest way to split a limited amount of money among a team such as the one you were on?**